U.S. Government
Q&A!

Why Does CONGRESS Have TWO HOUSES?

By Julia McDonnell

Gareth Stevens
PUBLISHING

Please visit our website, www.garethstevens.com. For a free color catalog of all our high-quality books, call toll free 1-800-542-2595 or fax 1-877-542-2596.

Library of Congress Cataloging-in-Publication Data

Names: McDonnell, Julia, 1979- author.
Title: Why does Congress have two houses? / Julia McDonnell.
Description: New York : Gareth Stevens Publishing, 2022. | Series: U.S. government Q & A | Includes index.
Identifiers: LCCN 2020033673 (print) | LCCN 2020033674 (ebook) | ISBN 9781538264355 (library binding) | ISBN 9781538264331 (paperback) | ISBN 9781538264348 (set) | ISBN 9781538264362 (ebook)
Subjects: LCSH: United States. Congress–Juvenile literature.
Classification: LCC JK1025 .M34 2022 (print) | LCC JK1025 (ebook) | DDC 328.73–dc23
LC record available at https://lccn.loc.gov/2020033673
LC ebook record available at https://lccn.loc.gov/2020033674

First Edition

Published in 2022 by
Gareth Stevens Publishing
29 E. 21st Street
New York, NY 10010

Copyright © 2022 Gareth Stevens Publishing

Designer: Andrea Davison-Bartolotta
Editor: Charlie Light

Photo credits: Cover, p. 1 mark reinstein/Shutterstock.com; series art (paper, feather) Incomible/Shutterstock.com; series art (blue banner, red banner, stars) pingbat/Shutterstock.com; p. 5 Cvandyke/Shutterstock.com; p. 7 (both) courtesy of Library of Congress; p. 9 Olga Moonlight/Shutterstock.com; p. 11 VisionsofAmerica/Joe Sohm/Photodisc/Getty Images; p. 13 Richie Chan/Shutterstock.com; pp. 15, 17 Chip Somodevilla/Getty Images; p. 19 Rob Crandall/Shutterstock.com; p. 21 ZUMA Press, Inc./Alamy Stock Photo.

Printed in the United States of America

Some of the images in this book illustrate individuals who are models. The depictions do not imply actual situations or events.

CPSIA compliance information: Batch #CSGS22: For further information contact Gareth Stevens, New York, New York at 1-800-542-2595.

Find us on

Contents

Words in the glossary appear in **bold** type the first time they are used in the text.

One Congress, Two Houses

Did you know that the United States Congress has two houses? No, not *actual* houses where people live. With around 535 members, those would be some big buildings! In government, a house (also known as a chamber) is a group of people who meet to discuss and make a country's laws.

Why is our **legislative** branch split into two parts? What is different about the houses, and what do they share? Turn the page to learn more about Congress!

Turn the page to learn more about Congress!

★ ★ ★ ★ ★ ★ ★ ★ ★ ★ ★ ★ ★

Government Guides

The U.S. Constitution is the piece of writing that states the nation's laws. It says "all legislative powers" are given to a Congress "which shall consist of a Senate and House of **Representatives**."

The **Capitol building**, where **Congress** meets in Washington, DC, started being built in **1793**. It has gone through construction changes, additions, and even being burned during the **War of 1812**.

Learning from British Rule

After almost 10 years of war, the 13 original colonies of the United States won their independence from Great Britain in 1783.

Toward the end of the American Revolution, leaders who favored breaking away from Great Britain created a constitution called the Articles of Confederation. This constitution gave important governing jobs, including creating armies and making **treaties**, to a Congress that represented U.S. citizens. This aimed to prevent an all-powerful government like Great Britain's.

★ ★ ★ ★ ★ ★ ★ ★ ★ ★ ★ ★

Government Guides

"We have been taught to regard [think of] a representative of the people as a sentinel [guard] on the watch-tower of liberty."
–Daniel Webster, American statesman

ARTICLES

OF

CONFEDERATION

AND

PERPETUAL UNION

BETWEEN THE

STATE

OF

NEW-HAMPSHIRE, MASSACHUSE
ISLAND AND PROVIDENCE P
NECTICUT, NEW-YORK, NEW
VANIA, DELAWARE, MAF
NORTH CAROLINA, SOUTH C
GIA.

WILLIAMS
Printed by J. DIXON &
M,DCC,LXXV

U.S. Continental Congress, 1777

John Dickinson of Pennsylvania wrote the Articles of Confederation. It named the 13 independent British colonies the United States of America.

The Not-So-United States

Under the Articles of Confederation, states had more independence. The federal, or national, government had weaker powers. Congress lacked the power to collect taxes from citizens, so soon the country was deep in **debt**.

In 1787, delegates, or those chosen to act for citizens of each state, met in Philadelphia to figure out a better system. It took months—and plenty of arguing—to write today's U.S. Constitution. Delegates wanted to be sure their own state had its share of power at the national level in Congress.

★ ★ ★ ★ ★ ★ ★ ★ ★ ★ ★ ★ ★

Government Guides

In 1784, George Washington, the first U.S. president, called Congress " ... a half starved, limping government, that appears to be always moving upon crutches, and tottering at every step."

Fast Facts on the Framers

Delegates who were invited: 74

Delegates who attended: 55

Delegates who signed the Constitution: 39

Delegates who also signed the Declaration of Independence: 8

Youngest delegate: Jonathan Dayton (New Jersey), 26

Oldest delegate: Benjamin Franklin (Pennsylvania), 81

Average age of delegates: 42

College with the most graduates among delegates: Princeton University (College of New Jersey)

Delegates who were **immigrants**: 7

Delegates with military titles: 8

State with the most delegates: Pennsylvania (8)

State with the least delegates: Rhode Island (zero delegates)

All of the delegates were men, and nearly half owned Black enslaved people—including George Washington. How do you think this affected the Constitution? How does this affect our lawmaking process, or system, to this day?

Finding a Solution

One delegate, James Madison, suggested the Virginia Plan, which linked representation in Congress to a state's population. The more citizens a state had, the more members—and therefore votes—it got.

Delegates from small states feared losing power to larger states. But larger states liked this plan because it let the **majority** rule. Roger Sherman of Connecticut suggested the Great Compromise that created a **bicameral** Congress. Membership in the House of Representatives would be based on population, but each state would get two members in the Senate no matter its size.

What went on inside the Pennsylvania State House (now called Independence Hall) as delegates wrote the new U.S. Constitution was top-secret—there were guards outside the door and the windows were sealed shut!

Government Guides

John Adams spoke for some delegates when he said, "Massachusetts is our country." But Thomas Jefferson insisted, "Virginia, Sir, is my country."

Two Houses are Better Than One

The Framers, or writers of the Constitution, wanted Americans to feel involved in their **republic** by both voting and serving as elected representatives. But they were also nervous about letting "ordinary" and "common" people have all the power.

The Framers expected the Senate would be made up of more educated, wealthy, experienced men—which is how they viewed themselves.

But what does the Constitution say about who can join Congress?

★ ★ ★ ★ ★ ★ ★ ★ ★ ★ ★ ★ ★

Government Guides

"I was excited and looking for a candidate to support, but as I kept waiting, I thought, 'What if the person I'm waiting for is me?'" –Xochitl Torres Small, Representative from New Mexico, on how running for Congress is open to anyone.

The House of Representatives was modeled after Great Britain's House of Commons. U.S. citizens elect representatives who serve areas called districts. In Parliament, members are called MPs (Members of Parliament) and represent areas called constituencies.

Parliament building, London, England

Who Can Serve?

All members of Congress must be **residents** of the state that elected them. Other than that, the two houses have different membership requirements:

(1) Representatives need to be at least 25 years old.

Senators have to be at least 30.

(2) Representatives' terms are for two years.

Senators' terms last six years.

(3) Representatives must have been U.S. citizens for at least seven years.

Senators must have been citizens for nine years.

(4) Representatives are elected by their district.

Senators are chosen by their entire state.

Government Guides

"The best plan . . . is to select a man of good sense, good habits, and perfect integrity [wholeness], young enough to learn, and re-elect him so long as he retains [keeps] his faculties [mind] and is faithful to his trust."

– James Beauchamp "Champ" Clark, Representative from Missouri first elected in 1892, on whom should serve in Congress.

Out of the 532 voting members in the 117th Congress, 144 are women. One hundred twenty-four lawmakers identify as Black, Hispanic, Native American, Asian/Pacific Islander, or more than one of these identities.

Making the Laws

The main job of Congress is to make federal laws. Laws are called bills when first introduced, or presented, by members in either house. Bills then go through many steps involving **committees**, hearings, changes, and votes.

Once one house approves a bill, it goes through a similar process in the other house. Then it's sent to the president for their approval. Every member of Congress has a chance to influence, or change, the bill—which means each state has a voice.

★ ★ ★ ★ ★ ★ ★ ★ ★ ★ ★ ★

Government Guides

"Congress in session [meeting] is Congress on public exhibition [display], whilst [while] Congress in its committee-rooms is Congress at work."
–Woodrow Wilson, 28th president, talking about where Congress' most important work is done.

How a Bill Becomes a Law: A Peek at the Process

1. A member of Congress introduces it in the House or Senate.

2. The bill is sent to a committee for review.

3. A committee may hold hearings on the bill, consider adding it to other bills or laws, or may suggest changes or additions.

4. The committee will then return the bill to the full House or Senate where further changes may be considered.

5. The full House or Senate then votes on the bill.

6. If the bill passes in the House, then it goes to the Senate for a similar process. If it passes in the Senate, it goes to the House.

7. If a bill passes both in the House and the Senate, it goes to the president for review.

8. A president may then sign a bill into law or turn it down, which is called vetoing it.

9. Congress can override this veto if the bill passes by two-thirds in both the House and Senate.

10. If Congress does not sign a bill within 10 days and Congress is meeting, it becomes law. If Congress stops meeting within the 10 days, the bill is killed in what's called a pocket veto.

As of 2021, most House of Representatives members made $174,000 per year. House leader, Speaker of the House Nancy Pelosi, made $223,500.

What Else Does Congress Do?

The Constitution gives Congress other duties too. For example, it can declare—or announce—war, **impeach** and put on trial officials who may have broken the law, approve treaties, handle taxes, and decide how to spend federal money.

Some powers belong to the House, others to the Senate, and still others are shared. Sometimes representatives and senators serve on the same committees. This checks and balances system keeps one house from having too much control. It also helps all of Congress to work together.

★ ★ ★ ★ ★ ★ ★ ★ ★ ★ ★ ★ ★

Government Guides

"... the Constitution makes us not rivals [enemies] for power but partners for progress [growth]."
–John F. Kennedy,
35th president, on advising elected officials to work together.

A job that belongs only to the Senate is holding hearings for people the president has nominated, or appointed, for the Supreme Court—the nation's highest court.

Room for Representation to Grow

Through the years, the House and Senate have been a team, passing laws to move the country forward. Their membership has also been changing. The 117th Congress is the most racially diverse, or varied, yet. However, white members still make up the majority, while other racial groups are underrepresented. This means there are higher rates of people from these groups living in the United States than are represented in Congress.

Many groups of people are still underrepresented in Congress. How do you think Congress can better represent all U.S. citizens?

Think About It!

What are the reasons a Congress works better with two houses? What are the reasons it might not?

Senator Sarah McBride became the first openly **transgender** member of Congress when she won her election in 2020!

Glossary

bicameral: having two chambers or houses

committee: a group that is chosen to do a certain job or to make decisions about something

debt: an amount of money owed

immigrant: one who comes to a country to settle there

impeach: to charge with misconduct in office

legislative: having to do with making laws

majority: a number of votes that is more than half of the total number

representative: a member of a lawmaking body who acts for voters. Representation is the way a person or group speaks for, acts for, or supports a group to which they belong.

republic: a form of government in which the people elect representatives who run the government

resident: a person living somewhere on a long-term basis

transgender: having to do with people who feel that their true nature doesn't match their sex at birth

treaty: an agreement between countries

War of 1812: war between the United States and Great Britain that lasted from 1812 to 1815

For More Information

Books

Foster, Jeff. *For Which We Stand: How Our Government Works and Why It Matters.* New York, NY: Scholastic Inc, 2020.

McDaniel, Melissa. *The U.S. Congress: Why It Matters to You.* New York, NY: Children's Press, 2020.

Sobel, Syl J.D. *How the U.S. Government Works ... And How It All Comes Together to Make a Nation.* Hauppauge, NY: B.E.S. Publishing, 2019.

Websites

Fun Kids
www.funkidslive.com/learn/us-uk-slamdown/difference-congress-vs-parliament/#
Learn about the ways the U.S. Congress and U.K. Parliament are similar and different.

Kids in the House
kids-clerk.house.gov/young-learners/lesson.html?intID=29
Let the Clerk of the House of Representatives teach you about both the history of Congress and what's going on within the chambers, or houses, right now!

Welcome to the U.S. Capitol
www.visitthecapitol.gov
Explore more about Congress and the building it works in through virtual exhibits, video tours, and fun facts.

Publisher's note to educators and parents: Our editors have carefully reviewed these websites to ensure that they are suitable for students. Many websites change frequently, however, and we cannot guarantee that a site's future contents will continue to meet our high standards of quality and educational value. Be advised that students should be closely supervised whenever they access the internet.

Index